FRIENDS

OF THE

REPUBLIC

FRIENDS
— OF THE —
REPUBLIC

SECOND EDITION

HARRY G. MICHAELS

TATE PUBLISHING
AND **ENTERPRISES**, LLC

Friends of the Republic
Copyright © 2014 by Harry G. Michaels. All rights reserved.

The opinions expressed by the author are not necessarily those of Tate Publishing, LLC.

Published by Tate Publishing & Enterprises, LLC
127 E. Trade Center Terrace | Mustang, Oklahoma 73064 USA
1.888.361.9473 | www.tatepublishing.com

Tate Publishing is committed to excellence in the publishing industry. The company reflects the philosophy established by the founders, based on Psalm 68:11,
"The Lord gave the word and great was the company of those who published it."

Published in the United States of America

ISBN: 978-1-62902-323-6
1. History/Social History
2. Business & Economics/Development/Economic Development
13.12.03

INTRODUCTION

This United States is in a mode of decline and we, as concerned citizens must speak up and express our own thoughts and ideas and relay our will for better government to those with whom we have invested the power of leadership. That is the author's intent and purpose.

Harry Michaels

—— PART I ——

DECLINE IN AMERICA

When World War II came to an end in 1945, historians were suggesting that the coming era would be called the Age of Anxiety because for the first time the human race had to face the possibility of nuclear annihilation. We did not anticipate the anxiety that would pervade this country due to the social deterioration of the post WWII era. However, we emerged from WWII as an unequaled world power and confident of controlling the nuclear genie. The United States had decisively won, perhaps, the most significant war in history and then began to reach out to its conquered enemies to help them in their recovery and reconstruction.

At the close of World War II in Europe and the discovery of the suicidal remains of Adolph Hitler and his new bride, Eva Braun, in a bunker under his Reich Chancellery, Germany was in a state of total destruction and collapse.

Then, in 1948 under the Marshall Plan conceived by General George C. Marshall, President Truman's Secretary of State, C-54 cargo planes from the U.S. were dispatched on a round-the-clock schedule flying into Berlin with vital supplies for the devastated German people, and helping them restore their shattered homeland to some semblance of order and recovery, while at Nuremberg Nazi war criminals were being prosecuted for unspeakable crimes against humanity. It was during this time that the full horror of the death camps came to light.

As a result of the Yalta (February, 1945) and Potsdam (August, 1945) Conferences, a decision was made by the allied governments to acquiesce to the Premier of the Soviet Union, Joseph Stalin, and his demands for control of east Berlin and eastern Germany at the end of the war. From there, it was rather easy for Stalin to annex the rest of Eastern Europe as well as the tiny countries of Latvia, Estonia and Lithuania. Other concessions were made as well to Stalin in the Far East. He was given control of the Kurile Islands and South Sakhalin Island north of Japan, the port city of Darien and Port Arthur as well as control of the Manchurian Railway. This was to be his reward for entering the war against Japan six days before the unconditional surrender of the Japanese on the deck of the battleship, Missouri, in Tokyo Bay. As an aside, it is interesting to note that in recent years there have been friendly meetings at some of the Pacific battle sites between veterans of the U.S. as well as those of the Japanese. A documentary was broadcast on American television over 60 years after the bombing of Pearl Harbor in 1941 in which a veteran Japanese pilot, who took part in the attack, was met by a veteran American pilot at Pearl Harbor on the Memorial of the USS Arizona, in which they recalled their part in the event—in friendship and good will.

After the Japanese surrender, General Douglas MacArthur set about establishing a new post-war democratic political system in that devastated country and the Emperor Hirohito was no longer regarded as a descendent of the Sun God. Japanese citizens could now look upon his face while they cleaned up the devastation of the war and the utter obliteration of Nagasaki and Hiroshima, the first two cities ever to be destroyed by nuclear weapons. Even though MacArthur was a political conservative, most of those working under him were liberal democrats who were following the deceased President Roosevelt's *New Deal.* This was in recognition of labor unions and the notion of collective bargaining to settle labor-management differences such as wages, work hours or working conditions. Generally, the New Deal allowed for private enterprise under the guidance of the government.

Back home, returning veterans had begun enjoying their rewards of victory by starting families and continuing their education on the GI Bill. All over America, college campuses were bordered by Quonset huts and barrack-type living quarters for married vets and their families. Young kids were now going to college with older veterans and could find themselves sitting next to a war-wise former officer or enlisted man from any branch of the Armed Forces. Adequate housing was quite accessible at a 3%, 30-year fixed mortgage or less on a VA loan. Things were booming as *Rosie the Riveter* relinquished her job for a returning service-man, and women went back into the home—at least, temporarily. New cars, toasters and refrigerators hit the market, and wartime ration stamp books went out in the trash. The price of a Coca-Cola was 5 cents. You could buy a new car for 900 dollars and a new house for $9,000. The cost of a postage stamp was 3 cents.

The United Nations Organization was formed in San Francisco in 1945, and its first major challenge was the Korean conflict that began in 1950. Communist-inspired Koreans from the north, who had seen the Communist takeover of China in 1949, launched an all-out attack on the southern provinces of Korea. It was believed that the incursion of North Korea, under the Russian-installed Kim Il Sung, into South Korea under the leadership of the American-installed Syngman Rhee, a devout Christian with a Ph.D. in political science from Princeton University, could trigger an Armageddon if nuclear weapons were to be used. A plan, therefore, of containment and resistance had to be implemented without provoking the hordes of Communist Chinese to enter the fray, and also to avoid resorting to nuclear escalation. With this delicate balance in mind, President Truman flew out to Wake Island (1951) to meet with General MacArthur in order to relieve him as Supreme Commander in Korea. President Truman believed that MacArthur was committed to launching a total invasion of North Korea that would take him into Manchuria, thereby inciting a major conflict with China. The new era, however, dictated a policy of containment of aggressive adversaries rather than the achievement of total victory and unconditional surrender as was the case in WWII. It was later to be learned that the containment policy of Soviet aggression, as fathered by George F. Kennan, head of the State Department's first policy planning staff (1947-1950), was intended to be political and diplomatic rather than military. However, the subsequent reconfiguration of this policy under the "hawkish" advice of Paul Nitze, National Security Council under President Harry Truman, led to the military involvements in Korea and Vietnam to curb the *domino effect* of a Communist insurgence.

As we entered the 1950s the Soviet Union, our ally in WWII, was now being seen as a deadly adversary following the deliverance of nuclear secret documents by Ethel and Julius Rosenberg (1951) and the subsequent buildup of nuclear weapons under Stalin's sinister leadership. Children were taught to *duck and cover* in response to an attack by the Soviets. The Strategic Air Command carried on 24-hour operations in which heavy bombers loaded with nuclear weapons were constantly airborne in rotating shifts. There was also a frenetic buildup of land-based intercontinental ballistic missile sites, and stealthy nuclear-armed submarines prowled the oceans on both sides. Then, in October of 1957, the Soviet Union launched Sputnik, the first satellite to orbit the earth, and as we heard the peculiar beep, as it circled the globe, the country was shocked into an awareness of how deficient our schools had been in teaching math and science. Movies such as *On the Beach* and *Fail-Safe* dramatized the cataclysmic possibilities of a military miscalculation. The idea was that any attack would be met with devastating retaliation, and so the policy was called *MAD* for Mutually Assured Destruction. Senator Joe McCarthy of Wisconsin was conducting *communists behind every bush* inquisitions in the U.S. Senate and many people in education, government and entertainment had their reputations ruined by association and innuendo.

Following WWII, Americans were said to see themselves as innocent and invincible—innocent in that we were on the side of righteousness and goodness, and invincible in that we were heroic and unconquerable. This was demonstrated in the television shows of the 1950s. The country seemed to revel in the innocent and naïve family life of *Ozzie and Harriet*, *Father Knows Best*, *Leave it to Beaver* and the most popular *Happy Days* as well as the invincible American hero western such as *Gun Smoke*, *The Virginian* and *Rawhide*. At the same time, a new form of irrepressible music emerged—the rock beat. Chubby Checker, Elvis Presley, Jerry Lee Lewis, Little Richard and Buddy Holley to name a few were giving music a new sense of emotional expression and displacing the dreamy, sentimental ballads of the WWII years. The Beatles were forming a style of music in Liverpool that was going to ride the crest of a social revolution that would eventually see its zenith at the great Woodstock *happening* in Bethel, New York. *Beatniks* of the 1950s were giving way to *Hippies* of the 1960s. Jack Kerouac and Allen Ginsberg offered young people a kind of ragbag philosophy of rebellion and alienation from the established American culture. Joan Baez took us back to a purer and more distilled time in American life in the form of rare-fied folk music and at the same time she and Ira Sandperl, her political mentor, established the Institute for the Study of Non-Violence in Carmel Valley, California in deference to the earlier Mahatma Gandhi movement in India.

As we entered the 1960s, there appeared to be a *Crossing of the Rubicon* of social change in the United States. In the major cities, particularly in San Francisco, drug experimentation and *free love* offered the illusion of creating a new world by *tuning in, turning on and dropping out* as espoused by the drop-out Harvard Psychology Professor, Dr. Timothy Leary. At the same time, a kind of psychological regression to earlier times in American history seemed to capture the imagination of the people. We lost ourselves in the folk music of Peter, Paul and Mary, the Weavers, Pete Seeger, Bob Dylan, and Arlo Guthrie—the son of Woody Guthrie.

When we traded in the sensible conservatism of Dr. Benjamin Spock for the *spacey* liberalism of Dr. Timothy Leary, we began a long slide into diffusion of the American culture as we knew it. A redress of the inequalities of the past among selective minority groups took on attitudes of hyper-atonement for specific historical ethnic transgressions. African-American militancy as espoused by Malcolm X in the South and in the form of the Black Panthers in the West emerged under the leadership of Eldridge Cleaver and Angela Davis. Mario Savio shouted and stormed at Sather Gate and the University of California-Berkeley campus became a focal point for crusades against the educational and political establishments while an African-American woman in Montgomery, Alabama by the name of Rosa Parks refused to go to the back of the bus. What followed were increasingly intense confrontations between the African-American people and white authority figures. A young visionary preacher by the name of Martin Luther King, Jr. took a position at the head of a movement for equal rights and non-violent civil disobedience and prayed for people to be judged on the *content of their character rather than the color of their skin*. In 1964, Civil Rights legislation seemed to promise a fruition of the *dreams* of Martin Luther King, Jr. and the African-American people and, at the same time, would presage the foreboding of difficult times ahead. Unfortunately, instead of getting King's message, the African-American society began aligning itself in distinctly oppositional camps and referring to itself, divisively, as *Black* as opposed to *White*. In March of 1991, a young African-American by the name of Rodney King was the subject of police brutality after a driving under the influence (DUI) stop and it happened to be caught on video by a bystander. The result was catastrophic. Resentments smoldered and then erupted in the devastating Watt riots of South Central Los Angeles almost tearing that city apart and Rodney King, himself, appealed for a cessation of violence in his pathetic statement, *Can't we just all get along*. In all this confusion and divisive anger, Blacks (as they preferred to be called) were invested with inordinate and indulgent deference while ignoring the fact that most all immigrant groups that originally entered this country or even those indigenous to it were oppressed in some form.

In the Black populations of America, there developed a bifurcated attitude toward American society. On the one hand, there were those who looked upon their U.S. citizenship as an opportunity to strive and to become assimilated into the American culture. They were to make contributions as responsible members of the society as others had done. At the same time, there were those who chose to revel in their rage and feelings of victimization. The latter groups were to present a huge problem because their demonstrated attitude of belligerence and hostility was one of getting back and getting even for the sins of the past and the battle cry was *racism*. Those who were to persist in this oppositional attitude seemed not to realize that their best interests lie in non-violent persuasion, as their great leader Martin Luther King, Jr. had taught, rather than in attitudes of paranoid hostility. The enslavement and exploitation of the African Negro was a terrible thing, however, Negro slavery was not the only form of indentured servitude in this country. Consider the plight of the Chinese, many of whom were abducted and brought to this country to be used to build the railroads in the west, and the Irish immigrants who built the railroads in the east suffered much the same indignities as the Negro—and don't forget the indigenous native American Indians who were so badly treated and demoralized that most now exist only in a state of helpless and depressed dependency. The Negro people were not the only ethnic group to suffer oppression and exploitation in America. It is true that no other ethnic group was brought to this country in chains and sold in a public square but we must also remember that the greatest suffering this country had ever known occurred during our own Civil War (1861-1865) in its struggle to emancipate the African-Americans from the bonds of slavery and tyranny. The subsequent struggle of prejudicial intolerance and racism that was to follow was a moral issue and a legal one and should have been dealt with as such. Once it became the law of the land that the African-American was entitled to the same civil/

legal considerations as the rest of the population, issues of prejudicial intolerance ought to have become a moral one and racism, as we have come to know it, ought never to have become a source of civil manipulation. It could be argued that legislating personal morality, social sensitivity and good manners is a pointless endeavor.

In spite of all the unfairness, however, with which some ethnic groups were treated in this country, some of their own served brilliantly and courageously to defend the United States in time of war. Reference the Navaho Code Talkers of WWII who made important contributions to winning the war in the Pacific against the Japanese, and the segregated Tuskegee Airmen (a group of African-American fighter pilots) who escorted bombers over Europe in a protective umbrella that was completely successful in fighting off enemy air attacks. Japanese-Americans who were imprisoned in isolation camps during WWII gave their sons to the Armed Forces who served magnificently in the struggle against the Nazi armies of Adolf Hitler, and African-American soldiers throughout American history stood tall with other ethnic groups in defense of freedom and the emancipation from slavery, and the right to live as free men.

In my view, however, indulgent acquiescence toward the African-American and then Hispanic groups selectively beginning in the 1960s threatened the integrity of what this nation had always represented, i.e., a society of hard-working and industrious individuals, by tradition, but also a society of well-defined cultural mores and idealistic values that we shared with each other as a New World culture in trust and community interests. This is not to say that African-American and Hispanic groups were inherently incompetent to hold their own in America but they did have a need for effective assistance and encouragement in the form of education and training and the opportunity to succeed. They did not need to be warehoused and custodialized in *projects* or administered to as helpless wards as in the case of the American Indian. Our liberalized *Great Society* programs only indulged and disavowed those particular groups as a way of dismissing the problem and perhaps atoning for a national sense of guilt.

The Great Society intentions were highly ambitious in a *social engineering* sense. It was intended to address the injustices perpetrated against minority groups with reference to civil rights and it did, which was good, but it also led to injustices toward those who were not allowed to compete for jobs because of *affirmative action* policies. Discrimination went the other way. A white person, highly qualified, could not get a job as a counselor in a community college because those jobs were given first to a minority person, who might have been less qualified,. This was because of the civil rights legislation that attempted to redress the discrimination of the past. The *war on poverty* provided aid to families with dependent children in the form of housing projects and money, and food stamps but led to, what some believe, was a further destruction of the African-American family. It encouraged women to have more children to get more money, and it encouraged men to shirk on their responsibilities to fatherhood and provide for their children. In the education area, many federal resources were channeled into helping the learning handicapped and preparing young ones in the form of *head start* programs, but it seems that money was directed in such a way as not to be accounted for, and that gave rise to abuses such that a school administrator would spend his allocation for the year on anything in order to not have his quota reduced for the following year. It also seemed to play into legislation to relieve home owners of paying a fair share of taxes to support the schools. Health legislation benefited many but most were older people on Medicare and those below the poverty line with Medicaid. On the other hand, the middle class working people began to suffer because of increasing costs of medical insurance. Consumer protection attempted to shore up deficiencies in business and industry, but gave people a feeling of having a *big brother* always looking down on you. Government seemed to be everywhere involved in our daily life. And, finally, there was the issue of the environment. The movement to preserve the environment was a good thing. We were hearing of polluted lakes and streams and waste dumps of hazardous material that threatened the lives of children but here, again, it seemed as though there was an over-zealousness that made it hard for loggers to cut down trees and regulate the forests.

In San Francisco, California, Enrico Banducci's *Hungry Eye* located at 546 Broadway Street was instrumental in starting the careers of Mort Sahl and Lenny Bruce, Ronnie Schell, Bill Cosby, the Kingston Trio, Vince Guaraldi, Glen Yarborough, Professor Irwin Corey, and the Mamas and the Pappas. It was *in* to take pot shots at the establishment, and the *flower children* started gravitating to the corner of Height and Ashbury. What began there as an innocent experimentation with LSD, marijuana and communal living under the pseudo-spiritual leadership of the drug gurus later became festooned with sickly flowers of hostility, disease and *bad trips*. It was a time of blasphemous defiance and misguided dissent. President John F. Kennedy was reluctantly sending *technical advisers* (1961) to assist the *Westernized* Vietnamese in the south with their struggle against the military insurgence of the Communist Vietnamese in the north. Senator J. William Fulbright of Arkansas and Senator Wayne Morse of Oregon presided over the Senate Foreign Relations Committee and daily made appeals to common sense, and the constitutional errors of committing U.S. Armed Forces to that Southeast Asia civil war. They further tried to point out that our military involvement in Vietnam would be very weakly supported by the Southeast Asia Treaty Organization (SEATO), and even questioned the constitutionality of our involvement in that alliance. All this fell on deaf ears because of the din of hysteria and confusion about stemming the *domino effect* of Communist aggression. The whole Southeast Asia situation put President Kennedy in a difficult bind because of his reluctance to fully engage U.S. troops in that emerging war. He had been burned by the *Bay of Pigs* fiasco in the early part of his administration and did not want to entertain any such future failures. In the 1960s, the Nation was in a state of extreme worry when it was learned in 1962 that the Soviets had installed long range missiles in Cuba that could reach vital areas in the U.S. The new President John F. Kennedy ordered Soviet Premier Nikita Krushchev to take them out unless there be certain retaliation that would likely lead to a nuclear war. The whole world stood on the brink of global devastation. Fortunately, the matter was resolved when the U.S. agreed to withdraw its missile sites in Turkey and allowed Krushchev to save face. A year later, in 1963, we were shocked and horrified by the assassinations of President John F. Kennedy and, in 1968, a promising Presidential aspirant, Robert "Bobby" Kennedy and a charismatic leader of the Civil Rights Movement, Martin Luther King, Jr. were also assassinated.

In recent history, the American culture has undergone a diffusion of what once were valued traditions. At the same time, attempts to redress the wrongs of past injustices took on cataclysmic sweeps of change. An excessive liberalization of laws and *Great Society* welfare programs provided special deference to those who would abuse the system or adapt to a further diminution of personal effectiveness and, at the same time, smolder with hostile/dependent resentment. Judicial systems and *due process of law* were indulgently administered to even those who had been convicted of terrible crimes against humanity, and were regarded still as invested with the same rights and privileges as the law-abiding citizen. Endless appeals and shortened sentences for *good behavior* gave the sociopathically disposed tremendous manipulative advantages. In my view, excesses of the American Civil Liberties Union provided criminals in court with rights far beyond equal fairness with an offended plaintiff, and prison confinement became couched with television, telephones, work-out facilities, conjugal visits, weekend passes and higher education in the Law. In some cases, even those who were incarcerated received Social Security payments under Supplemental Security Income (SSI). Criminal justice began taking precedence over citizen justice.

Radical and poorly constructed legislation was impulsively implemented to make things right and equal for those who were thought to be the most oppressed. Instead of upgrading the quality of schools in the impoverished areas with a plan of gradual and consistent improvement, Judge W. Arthur Garrity Jr. of the United States District Court for the District of Massachusetts, mandated that children from *good* neighborhood schools spend wasted hours on buses while being transported to *bad* schools across town. Instead of a well thought out plan of education and training for impoverished minority groups, we launched an indulgent welfare program that only served to further incapacitate and demoralize people. This only served to breed dependency and resentment in too many under-privileged Americans who could have been better served in more productive ways. Instead, we spotted African-American, Hispanic and American Indians with *affirmative action* advantages further lowering standards of achievement and productivity while at the same time surreptitiously labeling them as inferior and incompetent. Tokenism and mediocrity were the standards of those years. Some benefited, true, but we understand now that most did not.

Anger, resentment and dependency set the stage for a massive avoidance reaction with devastating flights from reality into a drug culture which had, in turn, unleashed the greatest social disorder this Nation has ever known as a new kind of violent crime was emerging on the American scene. Horrendous, irrational and incomprehensible assaults even toward children began occurring with regularity. Military assault firearms with rapid fire capability that were designed for war were being bought up and used regularly by dangerous individuals with criminal records because there was no effective control over these weapons. The National Rifle Association wielded tremendous power with their lobby in Congress and legislators backed off from taking responsible action.

During this time there was an excessive liberalizing bias toward justice for criminal behavior and the California Supreme Court virtually allowed repeat violent offenders to walk the streets and continue to practice their monstrous profession—and the rest of the nation followed that insidious lead. We had not learned as a society that some twisted individuals commit their horrible crimes *so they can relieve tension, feel pleasure and get a good night's sleep*, as one prison inmate put it. This kind of indulgent *liberal* thinking was to also devalue the quality of education for young people because it became the right of errant and incorrigible children to remain mainstreamed in the classroom. Teachers had to spend much of their valuable teaching time controlling those who would not cooperate. The threat of litigation hung in the air like a bad smell, and accountability in the form of increased bureaucratic paperwork further interfered with teacher effectiveness. In my experience, I discovered that school administrators found justification for increasing their ranks and their salaries. The teacher, who was the real professional, caught the backwater sludge and frustration that comes from a diminished status and impossible expectations. As classroom populations increased beyond the point for effective teaching, school funding started a progressive decline so that the younger, more enthusiastic and better trained who were the last hired might have to sweat out whether or not their contract would be renewed for the following year—even before they ever had a chance to make their contributions. The older and less effective were protected by tenure.

During this time, it became clear that disengagement from the Vietnam War was imperative. Our involvement had virtually torn this country apart and had come close to creating civil anarchy. In 1968, the Democratic Convention in Chicago, Illinois had produced scenes reminiscent of Nazi Germany prior to the advent of WWII. After the election of Richard Nixon in 1969, President Nixon and Dr. Henry Kissinger, Secretary of State had secretly orchestrated the bombing of Cambodia creating further unrest and dissent among the American people. That same year, Neil Armstrong, the first man on the moon, saluted the world with, *One small step for a man, one giant step for mankind.* The anti-war movement under the leadership of Jerry Rubin, the organizer of the Vietnam Day Committee (VDC) and Abby Hoffman (and the Chicago 7) played important roles in the disruption of the 1968 Democratic National Convention in Chicago. Then in 1971 Daniel Ellsberg, Pentagon military analyst during the 1960s, released the Pentagon Papers to the *New York Times* which the Nixon administration attempted to bar from publication by court order. Then on June 29, 1971, U.S. Senator Mike Gavel of Alaska entered 4,100 pages of the Pentagon Papers into the record of his subcommittee. This allowed the press and the public to see the real picture of what was occurring in Vietnam. All of these events as well as the break-in of Richard Nixon's collaborators into the Democratic Party Headquarters at the Watergate Hotel exerted enough pressure on him to disgracefully resign from the Presidency. Then came the *honorable* withdrawal of American forces in Vietnam in 1975 but which in reality was a humiliating defeat. We all saw on television the frantic scrambling for passage on helicopters atop the U.S. Embassy building as the United States Armed Forces evacuated Saigon. The degree of discord in this country over the Vietnam War had been horribly punctuated at Kent State University when students were fired upon by members of the Ohio State National Guard back in 1970 during a peaceful demonstration. We later learned that General Westmoreland and his commanders had falsified reports as to the status of the war so President Johnson could entertain a false sense of impending victory. It was later learned that Robert S. McNamara, the Secretary of Defense and the recognized architect of the Vietnam War later admitted that going into Vietnam was a colossal mistake. And so, for the first time in U.S. history, a President was forced to resign in disgrace (1974) for obstructing justice involving a common burglary. And all the while as we entered the early 1970s, we were laughing at the preposterous Bunker family that lived on Houser Street that put into some comic relief some of the important social issues of the day.

In June of 1978, the Jarvis-Gann Proposition 13 further eroded the financial support for the California public schools, which in the 1960s had been ranked nationally as among the best, but had fallen to 48th in many surveys of student achievement. Some had disputed Proposition 13's direct role in the move to State financing of public schools, because schools financed mostly by property taxes were declared unconstitutional in Serrano vs. Priest, and Proposition 13 was then passed partially as a result of that case. California's spending per pupil was the same as the national average until about 1985, when it began dropping, which led to another referendum. Proposition 98 required a certain percentage of the state's budget to be directed towards education. It could be argued that all citizens of California and, indeed, the whole United States have a vested interest in educating its young, and property taxes should be proportionately assessed to all land and property owners. It seems that the primary argument for the *People's Initiative to Limit Property Taxes* was that older Californians should not be priced out of their homes through high taxes. This could have been remedied by allowing a special exemption as they do in some states for the elderly and those living on modest incomes.

Even juvenile probation officers who had some leverage, in the past, to intercede with the incorrigible individuals lost that capacity due to the excessive liberalization of Juvenile Court Laws passed in California in 1961. Children were entitled to be represented in Juvenile Court by their own attorney—very often in opposition to those of their own parents. Civil rights became such a priority issue that even the mentally incompetent were released from institutional care, under the leadership of Governor Ronald Reagan (1967-1975), and put out on the streets to fend for themselves giving rise to a homeless phenomenon not seen in this country since the Great Depression.

The reluctance to address the problems forthrightly among our legislators, judges and parole boards had paved the way for unspeakable atrocities committed by violent felons who were freed to prowl the communities of law-abiding citizens and devastate their lives. The *new liberalism* had reduced government to a farcical drama without the will to assert itself in the interest of the common good. It had instigated rage among majorities and minorities as well. It bred a generation of poorly educated, poorly parented and poorly inspired subcultures who would seek to waste their lives in hopelessness and drug addiction, or to vent their rage and resentment in violent acts of vengeance and terrorism. Furthermore, the emergence of social discord and resentment had seduced the legal profession in a way that subverts its integrity. Though the practice of law as a profession is inherently a noble social enterprise that seeks to insure a sense of justice and fairness within the society, it has also attracted individuals with less noble character who, in the guise of nobility, have created further problems by generating excessive and greed-inspired litigation. Because of excessive litigation, the medical profession felt compelled to practice what is called *defensive* medicine which involved many procedures that were really unnecessary and very expensive. Likewise, there was also a reluctance of pharmaceutical companies to provide the new innovations of science and technology because they could be sued for enormous amounts of money if one of their products caused someone harm. The focus was not on the massive benefit but on the harm that might occur to a very few. From a social point of view, it did appear that over the past 50 years there has been a diminution of community feeling and trust among the people and a loss of confidence in government systems and government officials, themselves, have become discouraged and disheartened. No longer can agreements be honored by a shake of hands as was the custom in the United States for generations. Some of our best legislators have left government because they feel constantly frustrated to get important things done, and because the old comradeship of the Congress has been replaced by hostile partisanship and self-interest.

One of our most honored institutions, the U.S. Postal Service, which for generations had been a respected and dependable function of government, has become inordinately expensive and often subject to poor morale. In past years, those who delivered the mail were held in high esteem for their responsibility and service because every piece and letter was known to be important to the receiver but now it is so encumbered with *junk* and cheap advertising that its value has been diminished—while the price of a stamp keeps going up.

Women began asserting themselves and opting for equality with men in business and government. The concept of the *super mom* found a place in American jargon. Betty Friedan and Gloria Steinem led the Feminist movement and National Organization for Women (NOW) took extreme positions about the newly emerging role of women in America. Some advocated a complete independence from the domination of men escaping the yoke of submissiveness and docility, and engaging the world of men on an equal basis. The new movement made stay-at-home mothers feel intimidated and diminished while others, like Phyllis Shlafley, espoused the more traditional activities of women such as motherhood, homemaking and building character in their children while remaining the queen of the household. This revolution among American women seemed to confuse and threaten men who were emotionally unequipped to deal with such changes. Men began to search for solutions in all-male sensitivity groups in order to understand the changing roles of women, and to what extent they could assert themselves in this new context. As men became more sensitized toward women, women became more frustrated toward men. It became a very confusing arena of gender functions. This led to extreme reactions on both sides, and laid the ground work for such mating doctors as John Gray and his *Men Are from Mars, Women Are from Venus* books in order to lend some clarity to the issue and the whole nation teetered on the horns of this dilemma.

During the early 1970s, about the time of Nixon's resignation in disgrace, The Organization of Petroleum Exporting Countries (OPEC) had decided to put the squeeze on the American oil industry by raising the price of their products (1973) and causing unbelievable gas lines on the streets of America. Petroleum intensive areas in the U.S. like Houston went into a severe economic depression and many had to leave the area and look for work elsewhere.

On September 17, 1978, a meeting was held at Camp David attended by Egyptian President Anwar Sadat, Israeli Prime Minister Menachem Begin, and U.S. President Jimmy Carter as an attempt to bring peace between Israel and Egypt following several military confrontations. A peace treaty was signed on March 26, 1979. In the Middle East, the good will initiative of Anwar Sadat of Egypt led to the Camp David Accords and set the stage for the remarkable developments toward peaceful coexistence between the Israeli and Arab factions—an ardent hope that, unfortunately, was never realized.

In 1982, there began a softening of relations between the Soviet Union and the United States as a result of a letter to the Premier Andropov, written by a ten-year-old girl from Manchester, Maine by the name of Samantha Smith. She politely inquired if there could please be some way that she and her friends could grow up without the worry of a nuclear war. Because of her innocent and sincere letter, she was invited to spend two weeks in the Soviet Union among the children of that country. In a sense, she was the first female good-will ambassador to the Soviet Union. This was the first softening of U.S./Soviet relations since WWII. Following this event Gorbachev, who had been Andropov's protégé, assumed leadership when Andropov died and that was the beginning of the end of the Communist Soviet Union as we knew it.

By the end of the 1970s and into the 1980s, people became more sensitized to the vulnerability of human life and it was during this time that a consciousness spread across the land having to do with safety, environmental protection and life affirming health concerns. There were movements to clean up polluted lakes and rivers, toxic waste dumps, putting seat belts in automobiles and making cars more survivable and paying attention to diet and exercise. Medical miracles were beginning to happen frequently. In foreign lands, Amnesty International and the concept of human rights became a significant movement, and at home Greenpeace and The Sierra Club gave us a new appreciation of whales, dolphins and all living creatures (and trees) great and small, and at the same time a mysterious new virus among the homosexual community began making an appearance.

In 1979, our Embassy personnel were suddenly taken hostage in Iran following the defection of the U.S. supported Shah and the return of the Ayatolla Khoumeni. Foreign policy had failed again. Interest rates skyrocketed, further crippling the economy and public confidence. On the day of Ronald Reagan's swearing-in ceremony (1980) to the Presidency, the hostages in Iran were released. It was later discovered that this came as a result of a clandestine arms deal carried out by undetermined agents and allowed Reagan *plausible denial* of any awareness of the matter. Later, an ambitious Marine Lieutenant Colonel by the name of Oliver North would appear prominently in other clandestine activities surrounding the Iran-Contra affair. The CIA was also found to be perpetrating sinister plots to overthrow the Sandinistas in Nicaragua. Communism was being cultivated in Central America and that was not tolerable except, of course, in Cuba. We had been burned there as a result of the Bay of Pigs fiasco during the Kennedy administration and after the Cuban missile crisis we decided that we had better peacefully coexist with Fidel Castro hoping that with some mild embargoes his own people would bring him down. Getting back to Reagan, the super optimist, super communicator, whose denial of the *deep pocket* tendencies of avaricious people and his supply side economics enabled opportunistic entrepreneurs to pad their pockets with over-extended government funding. Many short-term jobs were created, erecting office space which was never used. At the cost of government solvency, over-extended credit provided enormous closing profits for the wheelers and dealers that probably set the stage for the hardships and *downsizing* of the 1990s. In later years, plant closings, hostile mergers and layoffs came to be commonplace events. As a result of the excesses of the 1980s, and the fiscal irresponsibility of the Executive and Congressional oversight committees who looked the other way along with Reagan's tax cuts and crash arms race spending, to break the back of the Soviets, we became the greatest debtor nation in the world whereas we had once been the greatest creditor nation on earth. For some people it was a time to make hay and jump on the band wagon of excess while plunging the nation into colossal debt and, at the same time, collapsing the old reliable Savings and Loan industry to the tune of $260 billion. It is true that this country enjoyed some years of prosperity and high morale. Interest rates and inflation came down under Reagan's leadership but a failure of governmental integrity and financial responsibility culminated in the loss of the lives of American astronauts and a beloved teacher in the disaster of the Challenger space shuttle when the urgency to launch under very adverse conditions and for political aggrandizement resulted in a catastrophic failure for want of an *O* ring.

The enormous nuclear arms race and *wild west* showdown with the Soviets did appear to break the back of the already disintegrating communist system. Reagan's single-mindedness of purpose in helping to defeat the *Evil Empire* will probably go down in history as his greatest contribution although the eight years of *Reaganomics* had tripled the national debt from $900 billion when he took office to more than $2.8 trillion at the end of his term. All the while, HIV infection became a frightening obsession because every day we learned of the skyrocketing escalation of this mysterious and fatal disease. While the AIDS epidemic began to jump to alarming proportions, excessive liberal persuasions provoked among homosexuals a wild and hysterical emergence from *the closet* and, at the same time, promoted, aggressively, a normalization and justification of the lifestyle to the public at large—and the AIDS epidemic rolled on. It became clear just how devastating this disease really was and never again would the word *gay* have the innocent and happy meaning as before. Even children now had to be introduced to the sordid facts of this terrible disease and its transmission. Childhood could no longer be a time of innocence and carefree exploration. It now became a time of wariness, hyper-vigilance and premature prurient knowledge. Tragic stories of innocent children being afflicted by contaminated blood supplies were beginning to headline the news and some were advocating a testing of the entire population and a sequestration of those who had been found to be infected.

It was during the closing years of the 1980s that President George Herbert Walker Bush and his advisers gravely miscalculated the will and intentions of Saddam of Iraq that, in turn, led to the very destructive and costly *Desert Storm*. During the Clinton administration that followed, the timidity and indecisiveness in the White House allowed for the butchery and mayhem to continue in Bosnia Serbia Croatia from 1992 to 1995. And when the Clinton administration took over in 1992, complex divisions of interests emerged which further accentuated the political differences between a liberal Chief Executive and a conservative Congress. However, instead of resolving problems and making purposeful legislation we got *gridlock* and mean-spirited antagonism. Issues that required the good will of the Congress as well as the Executive branch ranged from job creation and security, declining wages for workers (while enormous raises occurred in industry executive salaries and bonuses), minimum wage issues, the role of gays and women in the military, universal and portable health insurance, Medicare, Medicaid and Social Security, the moral questions surrounding abortion, *workfare*, funding and standards for education and what to do about crime and drugs, and don't forget gun control. We had become, by far, the most violent nation in the world and guns were the weapon of choice. Other more technical/political issues emerged as to the line item veto, PAC campaign funding and the power of lobbyists in government, the feasibility of a third party, taxation unfairness and complexity, term limits, balancing the budget, reducing the size of the bloated federal government and returning more power to the States to solve their own social and economic problems and, not least, ethics. Since Watergate, the government seemed to have turned inward upon itself to present, at least outwardly, an image of self-purgation and impeccable morality; that is, until President William J. Clinton's impeachment for sexual indiscretions in the Oval Office of the White House with intern Monica Lewinsky. Before he left the White House, President Clinton pardoned 100 plus convicted felons, before his leaving Office in 2001, whose offenses (U.S. Department of Justice) ranged from conspiracy to drug trafficking, to tax evasion, to aiding and abetting, to forgery and perjury. It was alarming that a President could get away with perjury, an indiscriminate pardoning of criminals, and setting of much more lenient standards for young people as to just what constitutes sexual behavior.

The great economic issues of the 1990s came to be known as The North American Free Trade Agreement (NAFTA) and the General Agreement on Trade (GAT) which some feared would further erode the standards of quality and excellence that had once been proudly shown on the label *Made in the U.S.A.* Ross Perot had given convincing arguments to the effect that passage of these agreements would cause a *great sucking sound* as many of our industries would rush to other countries where cheap labor was abundant, further depleting our own labor force and standard of living. Cheaply produced commodities would flood the American market and cause American economic values to further decline.

Our aggravating trade deficit with Japan in automobiles had embarrassed our own auto industry because they had let quality deteriorate and costs rise to where Americans were buying more Japanese vehicles. They were simply better. That kind of competition was healthy because it would seem that market forces would motivate the American auto industry to wake up and produce a better product—but it didn't. Our big industries were entrenched in their belief that nothing could effectively compete with American productivity. It would take a virtual collapse of the U.S. auto industry in 2008, and a bail-out of enormous government funds to make major re-adjustments in how Americanst industry viewed its true place in the economic realities of the 21 century.

Most would agree that it is not in the interests of the United States to isolate itself from the rest of the world, however, it must enter into world trade agreements with some control and moderation. The U.S. ought not allow the standards of a third world nation to uncontrollably subvert those of our own country and yet we must be aware that there are emerging nations such as China and India who are becoming more competitive due to increased focus on education and a workforce that will work for cheaper wages.

As an explanation for all the unrest and disturbances in this society many blame our violent culture, others our lack of religious training and taking religion out of the schools, others lament poor parenting, and still others political corruption and unworthy role models for the young. After all, we do see evidence of all this deterioration daily in our news broadcasts. We see children shooting other children in their classrooms and even crazed adults doing the same. In 1995, we all saw O.J. Simpson being acquitted of murdering his wife, Nicole Brown Simpson, and her friend, Ronald Goldman and then the cameras trained in on *White* and *Black* reactions to the verdict. The Whites couldn't believe it and the Black law students in Atlanta were overjoyed—testifying, again, to the continued bitterness and dissention within the black/white issue.

We see squabbles over whether or not to allow a judge to place the Ten Commandments in his court room. Parents seem desperate for answers to questions about how to raise their children, and television shows attempt to bring on professionals of one stripe or another to answer such questions. It seems as our technology advances, our social maturity is falling behind. We see violence and poor sportsmanship in our high schools, our professional arenas and even in parent supervised organized sports events for children. At the same time, ball players and entertainers are rewarded with enormous amounts of money while teachers and those whose responsibility it is to build a foundation for the future of this society in its young are barely rewarded with a living wage.

We would do well to reconsider the moral and ethical ideals that our forefathers diligently provided for us. They were based on the best of acquired knowledge and wisdom of western civilization. We have been ignoring, it seems, the pearls of our heritage and instead have been groveling in the domain of our lower natures. Instead of turning toward those baser forces and boldly confronting them, we have been turning away in the service of unrestrained accommodation and allowing the vulnerable young people of our society to become overwhelmed by the poison. William Pollack, Ph.D., in his book, *Real Boys* suggested that those who are the most vulnerable will break down first. It is analogous to being susceptible to asthma and living in a polluted air environment. Dr. Pollack went on to say that in our society boys are trained to establish a *mask of masculinity* and so repress their tender or feminine feelings. Boys, therefore, cannot express sadness, loneliness or feelings of alienation without suffering ridicule from their peers and even from their parents in many cases. Only anger and aggressiveness are acceptable.

So in the pall and confusion of disjointed purposes our government has been crippled and unable to resist the pressures of self-interest groups and *victimized* minorities. We have become so fractionated in consensual purpose that we have become a society ruled by the self-centered goals of special interest groups rather than *the rule of the majority* as was originally intended. Crisis reactions replaced long term and thoughtful planning. In my view, in trying to please everyone, the government has become an unwieldy, overfed, effete organism and the nation has become burdened with social disorder, cultural diffusion, colossal debt and undisciplined spending.

As the new millennium approached, people were afraid that computers that had not been programmed properly and would cause chaos and total disruption of financial transactions throughout the world. Fortunately, this did not happen and that anxiety was put to rest. Instead, as the new Bush administration took over the reins of government, the country was hit with a catastrophic event unseen since Pearl Harbor in 1941. On September 11th of 2001, a hi-jacking of four American airliners by Islamic radical terrorists crashed into the World Trade Center and the Pentagon, and flight 93 was heroically prevented from its intended target in Washington, D.C. by a few Americans who were unwilling to be commandeered by a few demented terrorists. Approximately 3,000 people were brutally and senselessly killed that day. In response to this tragedy, the Bush administration set out to exact justice in retaliation by dishonestly contriving a justification to attack Iraq on the alleged determination that Saddam Hussein was stock piling nuclear weapons to be used against the U.S. It was later determined that there was no truth in this assumption. The inner circle of President George W. Bush, Dick Cheney, Donald Rumsfeld and David Addington executed a war with Iraq with no pre-planning or circumspection as to how an occupation might be accomplished effectively. As it turned out, there was an insurgency uprising that would cost the lives of thousands of American soldiers and Iraqi civilians and set the stage for horrible episodes of torture.

For the next several years there was to be gross misman-agement of the occupation and a build-up of ill will against the U.S. throughout the world—and a loss of trust and faith in our own leadership and national purpose. Meanwhile, we became more embroiled in the Afghanistan situation and this opened up another war. The very sad thing that hap-pened during this time was that the *No Child Left Behind* bill that was espoused by President Bush during his early years in the White House was not financed as was intended in order for the Bush administration to finance the war in Iraq and Afghanistan—a congressional effort that would have had positive impact on the children of this coun-try, was sacrificed for Bush's unconstitutional war in the Middle East. The American people were once again told lies in order to justify an *unjust war* costing billions of dol-lars and a great number of American and Iraqi lives—and a consequent further decline in America's stature and moral leadership throughout the world.

President George W. Bush was re-elected for second term over John Kerry of Massachusetts, and New Orleans, Lousiana was hit with Katrina, a devastating and costly storm with great loss of human life and property. This all occurred because the banks and levees that protected the lower parishes were known to be incapable of withstanding excessively high winds and tides. Nothing was done about it by the Corps of Engineers who complained that they were simply not provided with sufficient federal funds to do the work. Before and, after the devastation, the Bush administration proved to be unresponsive and ineffective in providing relief services. Where was the *compassionate conservatism* when it was needed.

Many abuses of corporate management began to emerge and the real estate market began feeling the effects of Greenspan's warning years ago about *irrational exuberance* and razzle-dazzle sub-prime mortgage loans and *creative financing* that allowed people to buy expensive homes as a speculation that the property would greatly increase in value and then could be either re-financed (with anticipated equity) or sold at a great profit. In the 1980s and 1990s, Wall Street came under the influence of a derivative debauchery of essentially *betting* on the market with greater and greater stakes. A warning was issued by Brooksley Born, chairperson of the

Commodity Futures Trading Commission (the federal agency that oversees the futures and commodity options markets of derivative abuses) of a consequent severe downturn in the economy but her warnings were ignored. During her tenure on the CFTC, Born lobbied Congress and President Clinton to give the CFTC oversight of off-exchange markets for derivatives in addition to its role with respect to exchange-traded derivatives. Her warnings were opposed by Federal Reserve Chairman, Alan Greenspan, along with Robert Rubin and Lawrence Summers, whose economic philosophy followed that of Ronald Reagan and Ayn Rand in that *stay out of market regulation* and let the market regulate itself. It seemed that the country had been taken in by a pervasive sense of *getting it now* because for the present it seemed that America as well as the world economy was doing well. In recent times, Greenspan has admitted he was wrong in his economic world view and a recent ruling by the Supreme Court (in striking down corporate campaign spending limits) has again opened the way for further abuses of the system and Brooksley Born is warning us again of further downturns in the market until we learn from our experience.

In his book, *Free Lunch*, David Johnston reminds us of some important issues pertaining to our economic life in America:

- ☐ The power monger is no different from that of a cancer cell, which mindlessly seeks growth for the sake of its own self interest until it overwhelms its host.
- ☐ After WWII, our elected leaders worked to build and strengthen the middle class by investing in the brains of people, financing higher education through the GI bill, investing in science, education, public health and medical research and infra-structures.

- [ ] In recent times, we have turned away from these policies, and government lobbying and special interests have allowed the gross and greedy to impose their will over the middle class and those least able to bear the burden, thus subverting the foundations of this country.

- [ ] Other countries refer to their health systems as *health service* rather than *health insurance* as it is in this country. We do use a business model instead of a service model.

- [ ] Adam Smith tells us, *what improves the circumstances of the greater part can never be regarded as an inconveniency to the whole. No society can surely be flourishing and happy, of which the far greater part of the members are poor and miserable.*

- [ ] America ranked 36th among nations in its rate of infant mortality in 2006.

- [ ] President Bush said during the third election debate in 2004 that most of the tax cuts he sponsored went to low and middle-income Americans. That was not even close to the truth. In fact, most of the savings—53%—went to people with incomes in the top 10% over the first 15 years of the cuts, which began in 2001 and would have to be reauthorized to keep them in effect through 2015. More than 15% of the tax cuts went to the top tenth of 1%, a group that is over 300,000 people.

☐ During President Clinton's two terms, he gave the richest of the super-rich a much bigger tax cut than even Bush. Under Clinton, their effective tax rate fell by almost eight cents on the dollar, under Bush it fell only five.

☐ In terms of material well-being for children, the United Nations ranked the U.S. 17th on a list of 20 modern countries, right below Portugal.

☐ We now have almost three decades of experience with the idea that markets will solve our problems and the promises are not there. Many hundreds of billions of dollars have been diverted to the rich leaving our schools, parks, and local government services starved for funds.

☐ We pour billions into subsidies for sports teams and golf courses, a folly Adam Smith railed against in his day. Our health care system cost us far more than that of any other industrial country and yet we live shorter lives than Canadians, Europeans and the Japanese.

As the 2008 election year came upon us, there was a strong feeling, it seems, among the people that we, as a nation, were heading in the wrong direction and real change was needed in order to set the Ship of State back on the right course. Ethics, morality and trust in our society and government had been eroding for many years. We were sliding into what appeared to be a major recession or perhaps depression. Jobs began to disappear, unemployment started to rise to highs not seen since the early 1930s, and the U.S. auto industry started to hover on the edge of bankruptcy. The Arab-Israeli conflict continued to threaten the peace of the Middle East, and Iran posed a threat of developing a nuclear capability that would further destabilize the area. Pakistan, a nuclear power, presented itself as an unstable government and North Korea, again, appeared to be rattling its sabers. Amidst all this, the American people elected a young man of African-American-Muslim descent, who campaigned on *change* and was so elected. He was a former president of the Harvard Law Review and a man of vision, leadership and a will to restore America to its intended destiny.

After electing a *change* President, many Americans appear to be regretting the changes being implemented by the new President and want change at a much slower pace. Many are now espousing the need to move slowly because it does seem that when too many changes are made too rapidly and extreme movement is made in any direction there will be an opposing reaction—it seems to be a law of nature. The great philosophers taught moderation. Too much too soon of anything can lead to trouble and take us to places where "even angels fear to tread". This seems to be the major discontent with the current Obama administration along with what is perceived as a conciliatory foreign policy. It is interesting to note here that the Obama administration has done far more than the previous Bush administration to eliminate the al Qaeda threat.

However, our Ship of State has been far off course according to most, and moving it back on course would have to entail a lot of discomfort and upheaval. It is questionable whether or not slow incremental degree changes will result in enough credible movement to provide a stimulus for further changes—particularly with the apparent impulse of our Congress to deadlock itself in oppositional, contentious and partisan interests. Those politicians who have managed to ensconce themselves in their positions for many, many years seem to develop an investment to continue forming a web of personally advantageous networks. Knowing one's way around the *loop*, so to speak, has its advantages but also can defeat the purpose of good and responsible government. Perhaps if term limits for Congressmen and Senators could be re-established, as it is for the Presidency, the return to the concept of the *citizen public servant* would help the elected officials to stop basing their legislative choices on catering to the will of their well-healed constituency for campaign money and truly consider the common good of the country as a whole. Furthermore, the influences of lobbying in the legislature, in order to influence the special interests of those with persuasive financial power, tends to defeat the interests of the *common good*. Much needs to be done to restore the government to the will of the people rather than the will of a few. At the writing of this 2012 revision, it is the general consensus of the American people that our country is in a very dire situation with an enormous national debt that is rising beyond the capacity or will of our political leaders to control it, our very poor fiscal and monetary policies, the plunging real estate market and very high unemployment. In addition, there does appear to be an over-bloating of personnel employed in the government sector and that needs to be trimmed down considerably.

There is also the impending threat that large corporations will not hire as before because much of what is produced can be done robotically and those jobs that will be available in the future will require a high degree of technical training and education which our educational system is failing to accommodate. This country is becoming less competitive in these areas than China and India. It does, therefore, seem to suggest that a great focus must be put upon the sector of our economy that deals with small businesses and start up enterprises and improved education along with substantial preventative medical care for all because a healthy society is more apt to be a contributing and productive society.

In a recent book published in 2011, the authors Weidemer, Weidemer and Spitzer have written about what they describe as the *multibubble* economy that is threatening to collapse our economy and send the world into a massive economic *correction* that will create severe hardships. They are warning that we must be prepared because this is determined to happen. So, what is a bubble economy? According to the aforementioned authors, *An economy that grows in a virtual upward spiral of multiple rising bubbles (real estate, stocks, private debt, dollar, and government debt) that interact to drive each other up, and that will inevitably fall in a vicious downward spiral as each falling bubble puts downward pressure on the rest, eventually pulling the whole economy down.*

It does appear that greed and duplicity have become national virtues as competitive motivators for those at the top of the corporate and financial institutions ladder by *creating* incentives for the lower income populace to spend beyond their means.

PART II

REFORMING A
NEW AMERICA

At this time, in the summer of 2012, the U.S. is coming to another crossing of the Rubicon and it is believed that history, from now on, will mark this period as the sad demise of a great and promising new Republic or the beginning of an innovative and re-creative new adventure in hopeful and purposeful living.

In his book, *Come Home, America*, The Rise and Fall (And Redeeming Promise) of Our Country, William Greider quotes Adam Smith, founder of modern market economics, who was on the side of compassion. Greider goes on to say that, Smith was revered by economists for describing *the invisible hand* of the market place and taught that *moral sentiments*—human acts of *fellow feeling*—are the guiding forces that govern economics and prevent mar-

kets from injuring society. He further describes that empa-
thy for others, self-interested mutuality, and other moral
verities—are the things that Adam Smith taught (and most
modern economists ignore).

For many years now, government and private corporations
have been ignoring these ideals of our early American history and collaborating to skew our society in the direction
of a bifurcated populace of the extremely wealthy and the
extremely impoverished. According to author Holly Sklar,
the average wage for full-time workers in 1982 was $34,199,
in comparison (buying power) with 2006 dollars. In 2007,
twenty-five years later, the average wage for full-time workers was $34, 861. On the other hand, in 1982, when *Forbes*
magazine first published its annual list of the four hundred
richest Americans, there were only thirteen billionaires
among them. Twenty-five years later, the *Forbes* 400 con-
sisted entirely of billionaires and eighty-two were left off
the 2007 list because they were not rich enough to make
the cut. This great divergence of wealth is why families
have had to take on extraordinary levels of debt as they try
to stay afloat and keep up with mortgage payments when
their incomes are no longer rising. In 2005, U.S. household savings went negative—people spent more than they
earned—for the first time since 1933.

Since President Barak Obama was elected in 2008,
his administration has been dedicated to restoring a balance between conservative and liberal persuasions but

the Republican Party, from the start, has cast accusations that he is moving the country toward Socialism and they have opposed every significant bill advanced by President Obama or the Democratic majority. However, these criticisms dissolve under the most rudimentary examination of the facts. Firstly, Sam Tanenhaus, in his recent book, *The Death of Conservatism*, has stated that the decision of Obama's team to fortify the banking system and improve the flow of credit is, unequivocally, an attempt to salvage the free market. Fearful allegations that bailing out General Motors would result in nationalizing the auto industry had proven false. Secondly, President Obama's plan to extend health coverage to the nearly fifty million Americans who lack it is no more socialistic than providing Medicare for citizens over the age of 65. In President Obama's first year, it was no longer enough to oppose the Obama's health-care reform bill. They warned that it was a federal *take-over* and the Speaker of the House, John Boehner, recently commented that the entire Obama health care law ought to be *taken out by the roots*. At a town hall meeting, Bob Inglis, a House Republican from South Carolina, was besieged by angry constituents. One said, *Keep your hands off my Medicare*. Inglis replied, *Actually, sir, your health care is being provided by the government*.And thirdly, President Obama's foreign policy premised on diplomacy and multilateral concord, is as forceful a repudiation of the imperial presidency as we have seen in the modern era. All these are the actions of a leader who, while politically liberal, is temperamentally conservative, and who has placed his faith in the durability—and renewability—of American institutions.

Another example of the oppositional attitude of the Republicans in the Congress, it should be pointed out, is that in 2009 the Republicans objected that the Obama stimulus plan offered too little help to small businesses. But when President Obama, conceding the point, proposed an infusion of $30 billion to those businesses, with the sum drawn from TARP (troubled asset relief program) funds, Republicans instantly ridiculed the plan, for no apparent reason other than to deny President Obama a victory. The message of the Republicans is sheer stridency and opposition. Accusations that President Obama is a covert socialist were made by Newt Gingrich and Rush Limbaugh in the Conservative Political Action Conference in February of 2009. When the group re-convened the following year, it was Glenn Beck who summarized the latest version of the movement by saying that, *Progressivism is the cancer in America.* He went on to say that the Democrats were, *liberal neo-monarchists* and *would kill the very spirit that has built the nation.* Where are the reasonable conservatives today? Robert Taft believed in taking a stance of opposition and criticism although he supported Social Security and public housing and—overcoming his isolationist principles— approved both NATO and the Marshall Plan.

There is so much dissention today in our Congress with so little meaningful legislation. It is almost as though most Americans are resigned to an ever declining Nation with little hope of a resurgence of spirit and optimism. There is an oft quoted analogy of the frog that jumps into a pot of water. The frog is unaware that the temperature of the water is gradually rising and he adapts to the increasing heat until he suddenly realizes that the heat will kill him if he doesn't get out but by this time he is so weak he doesn't have the strength to save himself. I don't think this analogy holds up for Americans because any society of people who could summon the energy and communal effort, almost overnight, as they did during WWII to meet the challenge of survival can summon, again, the will and determination to capture the wind and set the lufting Ship of State on its intended course.

The following are a few ideas suggested as issues for consideration in re-creating America: *Only a single payer system of national health care can save what we estimate is the $350 billion wasted annually on medical bureaucracy and redirect those funds to expand coverage*, Himmelstein and Woolhandler wrote in the *New York Times*. Other nations have demonstrated that a nationalized system puts a lid on prices and profits, the main source of the perennial inflation of health care costs. The U.S. approach, in contrast to other successful health care systems, rewards the private sector and punishes the customers. The adversaries, to this concept of health service rather than health insurance, object because they think it is *socialistic*. This is a gross distortion of reality by catastrophizing systems that provide services and supports for all the people without disturbing the entrepreneurship of those who stimulate the industry and business of the country. Admittedly, the initial cost of a conversion would be considerable, but less than Washington quickly spent on rescuing Wall Street firms. An estimated savings would be $30 billion a year. It is interesting to note that during WWII and by 1946, the accumulated government debt had reached 120% of the GDP. Many people thought the nation would collapse under the weight of its debt and feared it would slide back into a depression. However, the opposite turned out to be true. After the war, the post-war economy expanded greatly and launched the most successful recovery the world had ever seen. This was accomplished, in large part, by all the investment in new factories and new technologies and instituting the *socialistic* GI Bill that allowed returning veterans to go to college and support the emergence of a stronger middle class. So, as WWII demonstrated, the reality test is not the size of the federal budget but whether the borrowed money is invested for the future.

The pension system is in very poor working order. This nation lives with an extraordinary contradiction. In an era when financial wealth has grown explosively, millions of baby boomers now find themselves approaching retirement with paltry savings and no pensions. They will have to keep working into their old age or accept a sharp drop in their standard of living. Social Security, the bedrock insurance for the elderly, provides income equivalent to the federal minimum wage. The old-style corporate pensions that guaranteed retirement benefits are fast disappearing as companies shed them to boost their profits. However, we can look to the many successful models. The Pension Rights Center proposes doing a lot of re-adjusting of the 401(K) system. A proposal was made for a new and inclusive national pension that, alongside Social Security, would require all employees to save in exchange for guaranteed portable individual pension accounts that would pay up to 70% of pre-retirement earnings. Furthermore, there are many successful models that use this approach and provide stable, reliable retirement benefits, including low-overhead, non-profit administrators with no game playing and no profiteering. Examples, include mandatory TIAA-CREF pensions for college professors, the construction trades, multi-employer pension plans jointly managed by labor and management, foreign systems like Australia's new national pension system, and the U.S. government's own Thrift Savings Plan for federal employees.

Restoring just taxation is a moral cause, but also a major step toward financing big changes in the society. A direct tax on wealth is considered unacceptable in American politics because, it is said, amounts to *confiscation* of private property.

However, home owners pay a wealth tax every year at the local and state levels— the property tax on their homes— and no one calls it confiscatory. The largest wealth holders and financial institutions could be offered a choice—either pay a modest wealth tax to the government or invest the equivalent in a list of innovative priority ventures or public improvements. There are so many ways to make significant changes and improvements in American political society we must ask ourselves if the status quo is really what we want for the future of our country. The point is that the nation must mobilize capital to undertake hundreds or thousands of large-scale, long-term projects to bring the unemployment rate down, provide substantial jobs, and invest in the future with structural re-construction.

Many people strongly objected to President Franklin D. Roosevelt's administration because they thought he seized too much executive power and with all his projects was moving the country toward socialism. The fact is that his administration set the stage for a victory over the Axis powers during World War II and a substantial economic recovery after the war. President Roosevelt enumerated a list of *rights* that would, for many years, be the textbook for political reform and social advancement. They included the following:

- ☐ The right to a useful and remunerative job;
- ☐ The right to earn enough to provide adequate food, clothing, recreation and medical care;

- ☐ Freedom (for businesses) from unfair competition and domination by monopolies;
- ☐ The right of every family to a decent home and a good education;
- ☐ The right to adequate protection from the economic fears of old age, sickness, accident and unemployment.

It was not believed that our forefathers intended America to manage the world. That is not why people from all over came to America. They came to be free of tyranny and oppression and the freedom to practice their better intentions and make a better life for themselves and their children. Unfortunately, the dark side of our heritage, also, manifested a mistreatment and brutality in the form of indentured slavery of African, Chinese and Hispanic people and American Indians. With regard to these groups, their full civil and social respect has been a long and difficult struggle but there has been progress. As someone once said, *it's not so much in reaching the end of a journey but knowing you are heading in the right direction.*

One could say that our global posture since the late 1950s has been undermining what made this nation strong including those constitutional principles that have been corrupted in U.S. efforts to prevail, aggressively, throughout the world. On the contrary, turning inward will actually make it easier for the United States to work out new relations with the other countries. Instead of dominating others, we can learn to live with differences. Instead of attacking foreign governments that deviate from the U.S. model, America can once again serve as a model of self-determination for all nations. In 1958, William J. Lederer gave us a heads up lesson in American arrogance by writing his book, *The Ugly American*, which showed how an overbearing foreign policy led to grave errors of judgment and foreign relations in Southeast Asia that we do not want to repeat again. Perhaps, aggression with guns and tanks and planes will give way to wars with cyberspace and technical intelligence. This means that our young people must be educated to meet those challenges.

In the last few decades, the U.S. economy has drifted further from the promises of the compassionate administrations, creating in its place a broad labor market of the underclass—temporary jobs paying unlivable wages and often filled with illegal immigrants. Guaranteed public jobs paying more than the minimum wage would permanently and automatically stabilize the economy, swelling the ranks of public workers in recessions and shrinking them when private jobs became abundant. Instead of punishing the working poor most severely in downturns, as the system now does, it would re-distribute the costs to all taxpayers to share as a public obligation. Real jobs would mean that reliable incomes would flow into those underprivileged communities, providing a concrete basis for economic development and neighborhood restoration as well as the redemption of damaged lives. If the job slots included school-age young people and men and women in the bleakest circumstances, they could suddenly become valued members of their families and the communities in which they would go to work, producing real improvements while gaining for themselves a foothold on the economic ladder. If eligibility were linked to continuing their education, young people would get practical on-the-job training and a strong reason to stay in school. Even the American military could provide expertise in training young people. Old sergeants know how to take unpromising kids and turn them into highly competent and disciplined young people.

Starting in the 1920s, there was a philosophy of that era, improbable as it sounds today, that was known as corporate liberalism. General Electric was the leading exponent of the progressive-minded companies. Greider points out that during the 1920s, General Electric was a pioneer in developing workplace and community relations that defused the harsher conflicts of labor vs. capital. Before government became a social activist, General Electric was already experimenting with innovations like profit sharing and worker councils. Its CEO even articulated a vision that someday workers would become the company's owners as the majority shareholders. Cooperation, General Electric argued then, enhances efficiency and sustains profit and long-term prosperity.

Other big names like Kodak, DuPont, General Motors, US Steel and Standard Oil also supported various progressive measures. Collectively, these elements fashioned the informal understandings known as the social contract. Companies would provide their employees with job security; industrial wages that rose in step with productivity; and health insurance, pensions, and other benefits, and inclusive bargaining would be the means to settling disputes. Not everyone in the country benefited, but the industrial arrangement became the core model for the postwar economy and helped create the large and stable American middle class.

The concept of *corporate liberalism* that was prominent in the 1920s with some of the great corporations was to reconsider the employee morale by insuring that everyone who works, whether in management or on the assembly line deserved to *own* their work, i.e. to exercise personal responsibility for what they do and enjoy the mutual respect and the right to contribute and collaborate in making important decisions and share in the profits. These elements of voice and status are very important to personal satisfaction in one's work. The most progressive companies encourage the cooperative spirit from top to bottom. Most people take a great deal more care and responsibility when they have investment of ownership and that also applies to one's work. Numerous academic studies have shown, and outstanding companies already understand, that collaborative relationships between top management and the workforce are more productive and profitable. The profits are shared because the workers are also the owners.

Our history of unions in this country goes back to the 1800s and the Industrial Revolution when workers were highly exploited giving rise to a more aggressive movement to unionize workers for their protection and decent treatment. The concept of labor-management relations had roots going back to the Protocol of Peace by Louis Brandeis in 1912 followed by the New York City garment workers strike that same year. Later, in 1949, Dorothea de Scheinitz published her work on labor and management in a common effort to reach cooperative understandings. Unfortunately, in the 1970s, it all fell apart. Major companies began to break the truce with organized labor (largely due to the aggressive stand of Ronald Reagan regarding the Air Traffic Control Patco Union issue) and also turned hard against the government. The Business Roundtable and other groups, allied with hard-right ideologues, were taking command of the Republican Party. General Electric, once again led the way, this time as the premier example of the harsh new bottom-line strategy that put corporations in conflict with workers and social values. Frank P. Doyle, General Electric's Executive Vice President, acknowledged in retirement, *We did a lot of violence to the expectations of the American workforce.* At that point, liberal Democrats might have reformed the regulatory system to make it more flexible. Instead, they retreated. With the election of President Ronald Reagan in 1980, the old liberal order was over.

One of the dominant themes of the decades from the 1920s up through the 1970s had been the reversal of the historic role of unions, namely, steadily increasing wages and benefits in order to share in the company's productive profits. According to Bluestone and Harrison, the gains in living standards driven by unions had been made possible through comparable increases in productivity and the result was an overall reduction of inequality in society. Then, starting in the early 1980s, an adversarial stance was taken by management to retrieve distributive gains that had been won by unions and their members over the years. Management used forcing and threatening strategies and was often prepared to use the threat of bankruptcy to gain the advantage. And, about that time, according to Daniel DiSalvo, Assistant Professor of Political Science at the City College of New York, he wrote, *Government-workers unions have been political juggernauts in the U.S. since the unseen collective-bargaining-rights revolution of the 1960s and 1970s. These unions are different and more powerful than those that battle owners and managers in the private sector. To advance their interests, unions in the public sector have created cartels with their political allies, mostly in the Democratic Party, to the exclusion of the taxpaying public.* In Daniel DiSalvo's book, *Government Unions and the Bankrupting of America*, he gives an excellent outline of how this aspect of a government takeover of public service happened and what can be done to protect the public interest.

On the private sector side, as we all know, corporations started to outsource factories and services and jobs to foreign countries thereby lowering their cost of labor. At the same time, management and higher positions in the corporations began giving themselves huge salaries, bonuses and *golden parachute* severances from the company. In the meantime, as mentioned at the beginning, the buying power of worker wages had not significantly improved over the last 25 years. On a more cynical note, one might think of what has been happening as the *rape of America*.

A full scale effort on the part of both private and public agencies must be waged through the willingness to invest in the future by creating the many jobs needed to reinforce our dilapidating infrastructure. As pointed out before, the vast investments made during WWII gave rise to the great economic recovery and sustained stability for many years. This must be accompanied by standards of equitable and cooperative participation in the direction, productivity and profits of our corporations.

One other concern of many Americans today in our modern society is the issue of Islamic immigration. There have been books written about the *infiltration* of seditious Islamic forces threatening our national security. I have heard and read reports that Europe and western civilization that was founded on Judeo-Christian religious principles are giving way to Muslim influences and Sharia law even though demographic studies show that France and Germany have the largest proportion of Muslims and that amounts to only 7 and 8 percent, respectively. It appears that there are concentrations of these cultural/religious groups much like other ethnic groups have formed in our own country. It is not unusual until generations that follow become assimilated and acculturated into the larger society. It is unreasonable, in my view, that a host nation would simply take a *live and let live* attitude while neglecting the establishment of social boundaries. In other words, it ought to be established that those who have come as immigrants respect the laws and culture of the host country. When Americans go to live in an Arab country it is expected that the Americans must respect the laws and customs of that country. It is only common courtesy if nothing else.

There are divisions among the Islamic people—the Shia and the Sunni sects. In terms of leadership, the Shia hold that leadership must come by inheritance directly from Mohammed while the Sunni, which represent 85% of the Islam population, take the position that leadership must be earned by proving oneself worthy and capable. These bifurcations are not uncommon. When you look at traditional Roman and Byzantine Catholic and then Roman Catholic and Protestant—Jewish Orthodox and Jewish Reform, even political divisions of reactionary conservative and radical liberal, there is an obvious tendency on the part of human nature to want to stay close to the familiar and traditional, on the one hand, and the desire to move forward on the other. There have been militant elements in Judeo/Christianity as in the Crusades and the Inquisition which was sanctioned by the Papacy. One could also point to justification in the Bible for those cruel persuasions and bloody seekers of martyrdom. My sense is that in Islam the militancy movement is on a much smaller scale than was the barbarism of the early Church. I am not persuaded that Islamic leadership is dedicated to the destruction of western civilization although there are elements that do—just as early Christianity sought to Christianize the world. Perhaps, Islam being a younger religion is also going through stages of evolution that Christianity has gone through. Reza Aslan, in his book, *No god but God* points out how different sects have interpreted the Koran in different ways regarding how men must treat women. One interpretation is demeaning and punitive while another is more considerate and respectful. In another book by Irshad Manji titled, *The Trouble with Islam Today*, she is urging those of her religion to reform the faith, empower women, encourage independent thinking and respect for the views of others.

So where are the roots of our political woes? It can be argued that the fate of our future lies in the quality of parent/child relationships and good learning experiences. Those of us who have studied Political Science and History as well as Psychology can see that if a child is treated kindly and with respect for his own personhood as he/she is growing up, that person will feel good about themselves and be inclined to move forward into the world with confidence and good will while, on the other hand, if the child grows up without positive regard or is an object of abuse of one kind or another, that child is likely to carry over its perception of the world as hostile and unfriendly and must, in adulthood, elect to take on the extraordinary challenges and struggles to correct faulty learning and experience or become an incompetent liability to others. In the latter situation, the child who does not feel good about him or herself will likely either turn against the self or others in some malignant way—and, in either case, that person will become a wasted human resource and be costly to the world at large. Our prisons and psychiatric wards are glutted with such individuals—not to mention those who plague the world with colossal exploitations. When seen on a scale of extremes we can note the brutal, exploitive, narcissistic bully or the self-defeating unproductive and unhappy recluse on the one hand or the cooperative, friendly and contributing member of society who raises healthy, happy and productive children on the other. On a lesser scale of extremism we can see those of a political persuasion who favor or perhaps need to stay on familiar ground toward the traditions of the past or those who are more emboldened to seek new adventures and knowledge. The social, economic, political community, therefore, must be capable of providing a government that enables all people within that society the security it needs in order to pursue its better intentions.

In conclusion, I would like to present a few more thoughts toward a reformation of our political-economic society:

We, the Friends of the Republic say:

1. The Federal Reserve Central Bank has not been working in our best interests and should be abolished and that private banks, with some competent State oversight, would better serve the people.

2. In the future, large corporations or small ones for that matter, should be held responsible for the consequences of their failures, either intentional or unintentional. We all have to learn from our mistakes.

3. The Federal government ought to be reduced to only the functions of national defense, inter-state commerce and social security. Furthermore, if all the money in taxes sent to Washington to pay for all the other government functions and bureaucracies were kept at the State level, there would likely be enough to provide free education up through the university level and free medical services for all the citizens of the State, as well as enough funds to provide for those unable to care for themselves. This is necessary to insure a viable and self-enhancing society.

4. There ought to be standards of social conscience and professional competence established for anyone

who aspires to serve in public office. A Democratic Republic is a wonderful form of government but it does have its limitations if the quality and character of the leadership is wanting.

5. There must be penalties for anyone who does not exercise their civic responsibility and cast their vote. When we see what people in less fortunate countries do to make sure their votes are recognized it makes us feel rather dismayed at the lack of enthusiasm of our own people.

6. The executive branch of the government has become so over-burdened with gigantic responsibilities and complexities that we ought to consider having two Chief Executives—one for foreign affairs who has some expertise and experience in that area, and the other for domestic affairs who has demonstrated competencies and understanding of those kinds of responsibilities. In addition, we might have a Board of individuals at the top who are chosen to represent the character and integrity of this country's ideals of honesty, fair play and good sportsmanship. The ethics and moral standards of our country in business and industry have been so dissimulated that our children hardly know what this nation stands for anymore.

7. Our leaders could become a bit more humble and circumspect so that we might learn from those in

other countries who have done better than we have in such areas as medical services. In an interview on the Fareed Zacaria program, a guest who had studied medical services around the world had discovered that Switzerland has had a health service system very similar to what is called *Obama Care* for the past 18 years and it is working beautifully for virtually all the people and at a much lower cost than ours. They call their system a medical service. We call ours medical insurance and that is because it is a competitive industry and much more expensive. It, therefore, must serve the financial interests of the shareholders and stockholders.

8. Lobbyists in Washington wield too much influence on the Congress and serve only the purposes of the large corporations. They are able to spend a great deal more money than most of us have to spend in fortification of their own special interests. This puts a great disadvantage over those of the middle class—the backbone of America—and those who have been elected by the people to represent them in a fair and equitable manner.

9. The income tax issue is a vexing one and deeply offends those of us who must pay large amounts of money to someone else to figure out how much we must pay the government because it has become much too complicated for even those of us who are

well educated professional people to do ourselves. Frankly, it's an abomination and must be returned to something simple as it was in years past.

10. One of the major keystones of any healthy, progressive and competitive society is education. In terms of priorities, it should come before sports and entertainment because of its ultimate value in preserving and advancing the viability of future generations of Americans. Education should not be politicized or bureaucratized but regarded as a true profession and those that enter it ought to be so regarded with standards of excellence the norm.

11. Our country is suffering from a lack of talented and capable leadership because of the extraordinary amount of money it takes to run for political office. It also tends to make political aspirants indebted for the exceptional financial contributions of a few. Furthermore, running for another term detracts from the time and energy an elected official ought to be spending at his job. I'm not sure what a better answer would be but it does seem to us that the broadcasting companies ought to be prevailed upon to donate some air time to a worthy prospective aspirant for public office since they are supported by sponsors that gain from the public consumer.

12. In view of the fact that people are living much longer than they were when Social Security was established,

it would be better for all of us if the retirement age was boosted up to 70 with early retirement an option at 68. Furthermore, part-time continued employment could be established as a normal pattern and that would allow those who have gained so much experience and skill in a particular occupation to pass on to younger employees and those newly entering the market place the benefit of what the elder people have learned. Another consideration is the fact that much of production and services are being provided by workers overseas, robotics and home office employment. It seems feasible, therefore, that the work hours be shortened so people can have more time to enjoy their families and for re-creation.

13. The issue of gun control in the U.S. is one of grave importance. According to *Wikipedia* sources (in the year 2000), there were 52,447 deaths deliberately caused by firearms and 23,237 accidental deaths caused by firearms. According to the Centers for Disease Control's National Center for injury prevention and control, the U.S. death rate from firearms in 2003 was 8 times higher than its counterparts in other parts of the world. We ought to realize that when this issue was considered by framers of our Constitution people lived in outlying and isolated farms and were vulnerable to attacks from outlaws, Indians, wild animals and even British sympathizers. It made sense

for people who lived in those times to have some way of defending themselves. Today, however, we live in a civilized society protected by police forces and legal prohibitions—at least this is what is intended. We must take firearms (and especially those that are intended for war) out of the hands of those who are incapable of handling them responsibly—or at least, as Senator Moynihan once said in 1993, *if we can't control guns at least let us tax bullets and ammunition or set standards on who are allowed to purchase them.* The other alternative, as suggested by John R. Lott, Jr. in his 1998 publication *More Guns—Less Crime*, is to legally allow all citizens to carry firearms as a protection against those who would be a threat.

14. Finally, the beauty of our system is that our forefathers understood that nothing is perfect so they designed our form of government to be changeable and improvable as the knowledge and awareness of the people evolves and grows. It is based on the premise that reasonable people of good will can sit down together with differing views and persuasions and talk sensibly about a consensual course of action for the betterment of all. With the sincere input of the leaders, one can determine which confluence of ideas will likely give the best results for the needed choices and directions.

In addition, we do not want to omit the wise recommendations of Warren Buffet who, in a recent interview with CNBC, offered persuasive reform measures in his Congressional Reform Act of 2012 as follows:

1. No tenure/no pension: Congress men and women collect a salary while in office and receive no pay when they are out of office.

2. Congress (past, present & future) participates in Social Security: All funds in the Congressional retirement fund move to the Social Security system immediately. All future funds flow into the Social Security system, and Congress participates with the American people. It may not be used for any other purpose.

3. Congress can purchase their own retirement plan, just as all Americans do.

4. Congress will no longer vote themselves a pay raise. Congressional pay will rise by the lower of CPI or 3%.

5. Congress will lose their current health care system. They must participate in the same health care system as the American people.

6. Congress must equally abide by all laws they impose on the American people.

7. All contracts with past and present Congress men and women are void effective 12/1/12. The American people did not make these contracts with Congress

men or women. Congress made all these contracts with themselves.

And he said in closing, *Serving in Congress is an honor, not a career. The Founding Fathers envisioned citizen legislators, so ours should serve their term(s), then go home and back to work.*

Isn't it time we cleaned house and thought about new guidelines for our country's future? Let's all express our thoughts and feelings to the politicians in Washington and let them know the will of the people. Could it be a time to consider a third party?

hgm1931@gmail.com

BIBLIOGRAPHY

Aslan, Reza (2006). No god but God: The origins, evolution and future of Islam. New York: Random House, Inc.

Baker, Russ (2009). *Family of Secrets: The Bush dynasty, the powerful forces that put it in the White House, and what their influence means for America*. New York: Bloomsbury Press.

Beven, Gerald, translator (2003). *Alexis de Tocqueville, Democracy in America*. New York: Penguin Classics.

Blackmon, Douglas A. (2008). *Slavery by Another Name: The re-enslavement of Black Americans from the Civil War to World War II*. New York: Anchor Books.

Bork, Robert H. (1996). *Slouching Toward Gomorrah: Modern Liberalism and American Decline*. New York: Regan Books.

Bradley, Bill (2007). *The New American Story*. New York: Random House.

Brzezinski, Zbigniew (2012). *Strategic Vision*. New York: Basic Books.

Buchanan, Patrick J. (2006). *State of Emergency: The third world invasion and conquest of America*. New York: Thomas Dunne Books.

Coontz, Stephanie (1992). *The Way We Never Were: American families and the nostalgia trap*. New York: Basic Books.

DiSalvo, Daniel (2011). *Government Unions and the Bankruptcy of America*. New York: Encounter Books.

Donald, David Herbert (1995). *Lincoln*. New York: Simon & Schuster.

Dorgan, Senator Byron L. (2006). *Take This Job and Ship It: How corporate greed and brain dead politics are selling out America*. New York: Thomas Dunn Books.

Draut, Tamara (2005). *Strapped: Why America's 20- and 30-somethings can't get ahead*. New York: Doubleday.

Dray, Philip (2010). *There is Power in a Union*. New York: First Anchor Books.

Ellis, Joseph J. (2007). *American Creation*. New York: Alfred A. Knoff.

Eirkson, Erik (1950). *Childhood and Society.* New York: W.W. Norton & Co.

Fisk, Robert (2007). *The Great War for Civilization:* The conquest of the Middle East. New York: Vantage Press.

Freddoso, David (2008). *The Case Against Barak Obama: The unlikely rise and unexamined agenda of the media's favorite candidate.* Washington, D.C.: Regnery Publishing Co.

Friedman, Thomas L. (2005). *The World is Flat: A brief history of the 21st century.* New York: Farrar, Straus and Giroux.

Frost, S. E., Jr. (1989). *Basic Teachings of the Great Philosophers.* New York: Anchor Books.

Gabriel, Brigitte (2006). *Because They Hate: A survivor of Islamic terror warns America.* New York: St. Martin's Press.

Gingrich, Newt (2008). *Real Change: From the world that fails to the world that works.* New York: Warner Books, Inc.

Goodwin, Doris Kearns (1994). *No Ordinary Time. Franklin and Eleanor Roosevelt: The home front in WWII.* New York: Simon & Schuster Paperback

Greider, William (2009). *Come Home, America: The rise and fall (and redeeming promise) of our country.* New York: Rodale, Inc.

Iococca, Lee (2007). *Where Have All The Leaders Gone?* New York: Scribner, Inc.

Iserbyt, Charlotte Thomson (1999). *The Dumbing Down of America.* Ravenna, OH: Conscience Press.

Johnston, David Cay (2008). *Free Lunch: How the wealthiest Americans enrich themselves at government expense (and stick you with the bill).* New York: Penguin Group.

Kennan, George F. (1972). *Memoirs 1950-1963.* New York: Pantheon Books.

Lederer, William J. and Burdick, Eugene (1965). *The Ugly American.* New York: W.W. Norton & Co. Paperback.

Lott, John R., Jr. (1998). *More Guns Less Crime: Understanding crime and gun control laws.* Chicago, IL: University of Chicago Press.

Manji, Irshad (2003). *The Trouble with Islam Today.* New York: St. Martin's Press. McCullough, David (2005). *1776.* New York: Simon & Shuster.

McGreal, Ian P., (Ed.) (1992). *Great Thinkers of the Western World:* The major ideas and classic works of more than 100 outstanding Western philosophers, physical and social scientists, psychologists, religious writers, and theologians. New York: HarperCollins Publishers, Inc.

Moyers, Bill (2011). *Bill Moyers Journal.* New York: The New Press.

Nolte, Dorothy Law (1998). *Children Learn What They Live.* New York: Workman Publishing Company, Inc.

Obama, Barak (1995). *Dreams From My Father.* New York: Broadway Paperbacks.

Obama, Barak (2006). *The Audacity of Hope.* New York: Crown Publishers.

Obama, Barak (2008). *Change You Can Believe In.* New York: Three Rivers Press.

Roberts, J. M. (1993). *A Short History of the World.* New York: Oxford University.

Smith, Adam (2009). *The Wealth of Nations.* A Digireads. com Book.

Spencer, Robert (2008). *Stealth Jihad: How radical Islam is subverting America.* Washington, D.C.: Regnery Publishing, Inc.

Sperry, Paul (2005). *Infiltration: How Muslim spies and subversives have penetrated Washington.* Nashville, TN: Nelson Current.

Tanenhaus, Sam (2009). *The Death of Conservatism: A movement and its consequences.* New York: Random House.

Taylor, Maxwell D., General of the Army (1972). *Swords and Plowshares: A memoir*. New York: De Capo Press.

Tett, Gillian (2009). *Fool's Gold: How the bold dream of a small tribe at J.P. Morgan was corrupted by Wall Street greed and unleashed a catastrophe*. New York: Free Press.

Thompson, Nicholas (2009). *The Hawk and the Dove:* Paul Nitze, George Kennan, and the history of the cold war. New York: Henry Holt & Co.

Thoreau, Henry David (1993). *Walden and Other Writings*. New York: Barnes & Noble, Inc.

Updike, John (2006). *Terrorist.* New York: Alfred A. Knopf.

Webb, Jim (2008). *A Time to Fight*. New York: Broadway Books.

Wills, Garry (2010). *Bomb Power: The modern presidency and the national security state*. New York: The Penguin Press.